W9-AJS-528

EAST NORTHPORT PUBLIC LIBRARY
EAST NORTHPORT, NEW YORK

Counting in the Biomes

Counting in the
Desert

Fredrick L. McKissack, Jr. and Lisa Beringer McKissack

Enslow Elementary

an imprint of

 Enslow Publishers, Inc.

40 Industrial Road
Box 398
Berkeley Heights, NJ 07922
USA

http://www.enslow.com

To Patricia and Fred McKissack, Sr.
Thank you. For everything.

Enslow Elementary, an imprint of Enslow Publishers, Inc.

Enslow Elementary® is a registered trademark of Enslow Publishers, Inc.

Copyright © 2008 by Enslow Publishers, Inc.

All rights reserved.

No part of this book may be reproduced by any means without the written permission of the publisher.

Library of Congress Cataloging-in-Publication Data

McKissack, Fredrick, Jr.
    Counting in the desert / Fredrick L. McKissack, Jr. and Lisa Beringer McKissack.
      p. cm. — (Counting in the biomes)
    Summary: "Children can count from one to ten as they read about the different animals, plants, and features of the desert"—Provided by publisher.
    Includes bibliographical references and index.
    ISBN-13: 978-0-7660-2988-0
    ISBN-10: 0-7660-2988-3
    1. Counting—Juvenile literature. 2. Desert animals—Juvenile literature. 3. Desert ecology—Juvenile literature. 4. Deserts—Juvenile literature. 5. Biotic communities—Juvenile literature. I. McKissack, Lisa Beringer. II. Title.
    QA113.M39653 2008
    578.754—dc22
                              2007020288

Printed in the United States of America

10 9 8 7 6 5 4 3 2 1

To Our Readers: We have done our best to make sure all Internet Addresses in this book were active and appropriate when we went to press. However, the author and the publisher have no control over and assume no liability for the material available on those Internet sites or on other Web sites they may link to. Any comments or suggestions can be sent by e-mail to comments@enslow.com or to the address on the back cover.

Every effort has been made to locate all copyright holders of material used in this book. If any errors or omissions have occurred, corrections will be made in future editions of this book.

Illustration Credits: Paul G. Adam/Photo Researchers, Inc., pp. 3 (cactus), 25 (inset), 29 (cactus); © Alain Dragesco-Joffe/Animals Animals-Earth Sciences, pp. 3 (scorpion), 8–9, 28 (scorpion); Enslow Publishers, Inc., p. 4 (map); Bryan Firestone/Shutterstock, pp. 2, 10 (inset); Courtesy of Florida Division of Plant Industries Archives, Florida Department of Agriculture and Consumer Services, United States, pp. 3 (spider), 21, 28–29 (background), 29 (spider), 30–31 (background), 32 (background); © image100/SuperStock, pp. 3 (ostrich), 23, 29 (ostrich); © 2007 jupiterimages.com, p. 19 (inset); Craig K. Lorenz/PhotoResearchers, Inc., pp. 19, 29 (bighorn sheep); © Joe McDonald/Visuals Unlimited, pp. 3 (sand dune), 13 (top), 27 (top); Vladimir Melnik/Shutterstock, pp. 1, 3 (background), 4–5 (background), 10–11 (background), 12–13 (background), 18–19 (background), 20–21 (background), 22–23 (background), 26–27 (background); © Marli Miller/Visuals Unlimited, p. 13 (bottom); Mike Norton/Shutterstock, pp. 5, 24–25 (background), 26; Vova Pomortzeff/Shutterstock, pp. 3 (camel), 6–7, 10–11, 28 (Sahara desert), 28 (camel); Leonard Lee Rue III / Photo Researchers, Inc., pp. 3 (kangaroo), 14–15, 28 (kangaroo); kristian_sekulic/Shutterstock, p. 22; U.S. Fish and Wildlife Service, pp. 16–17, 27 (bottom), 29 (roadrunner); © Jim Wark/Visuals Unlimited, pp. 13 (middle), 28 (star-shaped sand dune); Warren Photographic, p. 12.

Cover Illustration: © Alain Dragesco-Joffe/Animals Animals-Earth Sciences.

Contents

Where in the world are the deserts?

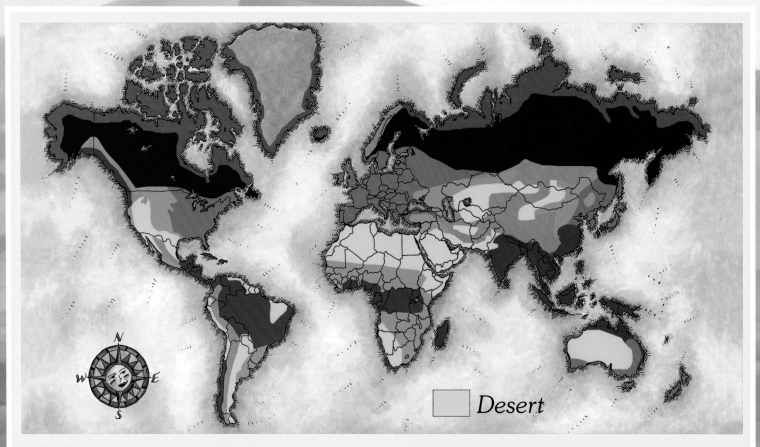

Desert

What is a biome? A biome is an area of land or water with special plants and animals that need each other to live. There are many different kinds of biomes. Each biome has different kinds of weather.

In this book you will find out all about a place called the desert.

desert (DEZ-ert)—A biome with very little rain and very few plants. Many people think deserts are hot and sandy, but they can be cold and icy, too! The tundra is a cold desert.

sand dunes—A mound of sand formed by the wind. There are four types of sand dunes. Each has a different shape and is made by the wind.

How many hottest deserts are there in the world?

One

Deserts come in different sizes. **One** desert is bigger than all the rest. The Sahara (suh-HAIR-ah) desert is the biggest hot desert in the world. It is in North Africa. The Sahara is almost as big as the United States.

The Sahara is also the hottest desert. During the day, it gets very hot. At night, it can get very cold.

1

How many **claws** does a **scorpion** have on its front legs?

Two

There are many different animals in the desert. The scorpion (SCORE-pea-in) has **two** claws on its front legs. It uses them to catch and kill other animals for food. Scorpions look for food at night when the desert is cool. This helps them keep water in their bodies. The cool night means scorpions need to use less water.

How many camels do you see?

Three

Camels help people move things in the desert. **Three** camels walking in a caravan (KAR-eh-van), or a long line, carry many different things. They might carry food, water, tools, or even people as they make their way across the desert.

Camels are not fast walkers, but they are very strong. They can carry 1,000 pounds. That is about the size of a big pickup truck. Lucky for them, camels can go a long time without water. This is important in the desert.

How many types of sand dunes are there?

Four

Because deserts are very dry, wind blows sand around. The wind makes sand dunes. There are **four** kinds of sand dunes found in a desert.

1. One kind of sand dune is long and thin. It can stretch for up to 250 miles. It would take four hours to drive that far on a highway.

2. A sand dune can look like a half-moon. They are made in parts of the desert with very little sand.

3. Another kind of sand dune is star-shaped. These dunes are made by wind coming from four different directions.

4. The last kind of sand dune is long and flat. One end is bigger than the other.

How many **kangaroos** in a **group**?

Five

    The desert can be a hard place to live. Some animals live in groups to stay safe. The red kangaroo lives in groups of about **five**. Most groups are made up of mother and baby kangaroos. A few father kangaroos may live with them too. Living in groups helps them. One mother kangaroo will watch all the babies while the other mothers look for food and water. Red kangaroos can go for months without water if they have to.

How many **tail feathers** does this **roadrunner** have?

Six

Many different birds are found in the desert. This roadrunner has **six** tail feathers. The roadrunner is brown and white and has a long tail.

Roadrunners are very fast birds. Like other animals in the desert, roadrunners need water. Their bodies do a good job of keeping water inside. And they rest most of the day when the sun is very hot.

How many **bighorn sheep** do you **see**?

Seven

Another desert animal that lives in a group is the bighorn sheep. They live in groups of about **seven**. During the hot and dry summer, they live in the mountains. When it gets too cold, they move to the desert. Bighorn sheep need water every few days when they live in the desert. Living in a group can help them find water faster.

How many **legs** does a recluse spider have?

Eight

There are many different spiders that live in the desert. The recluse (REK-loose) spider has **eight** very long legs. It is a very shy spider. It looks for food at night and hides during the day. Most recluse spiders will hide under rocks. The recluse spider is another animal that can go for many days without water.

21

How many ostriches do you see?

Nine

The ostrich (AWS-trich) is the biggest bird in the world. It is too big to fly. Ostriches like living with others. They live in groups of about **nine**. Each bird helps look out for the others. They look around for animals that may want to eat them. If they see one, they all run away. The ostrich does not need water in the desert. They get all the water they need from the food they eat.

How many arms does this saguaro cactus have?

Ten

The saguaro cactus (seh-gwa-ROE CACK-tuhs) is the biggest cactus in the desert. This one has **ten** arms! The cactus is very thick and very tall. They can weigh up to **ten** tons. That is almost as heavy as a semitrailer truck.

The saguaro cactus needs lots of water to live. It grows roots deep into the ground where water is stored.

More Information on Deserts

Note to Parents and Teachers: Read this section together. Some words or concepts may need to be explained.

A desert is the driest of all biomes. A desert gets less than ten inches of water a year. Most plants and animals that live in the desert need very little water to live.

Some plants and animals store water in their bodies. Desert plants like the cactus grow thick waxy leaves that help store water. They also grow needlelike spines that keep animals from eating them. Like the cactus, some animals and spiders can keep water in their bodies too.

After it rains, water is stored deep underground. It is held in layers of rocks and soil. Plants and animals can find it when they need water. Some animals

dig deep into the ground to find the water. Some plants have very long roots that grow deep into the ground. They can store water in their roots for the dry days.

Some deserts have large rivers that snake across the land. Others have large lakes. But this is very rare. Deserts with rivers or lakes have lots of different plants and animals living nearby.

Deserts are found all over the world. Each one is different. Some deserts are rocky. Others are sandy. Some deserts are flat. Still others are high in the mountains. And some deserts are cold.

One thing all deserts have in common is that they are very dry. They also have a lot of neat things to count. Here are some things you can count in a desert.

Count Again!

1		One
2		Two
3		Three
4		Four
5		Five

Count Again!

6		Six
7		Seven
8		Eight
9		Nine
10		Ten

Words to Know

caravan—A long line of animals and people walking.

recluse—Someone or something that is shy and lives alone.

roots—Part of a plant that grows under the ground.

sand dune—A big pile of sand.

scorpion—An animal that looks like a spider with a tail.

spine—A needle that sticks out of cactus leaves.

ton—A very heavy weight. 2,000 pounds = 1 ton. One elephant can weight about four tons!

Learn More

Books

Gaff, Jackie. *I Wonder Why the Sahara is Cold at Night, and Other Questions About Deserts*. Boston, Mass.: Kingfisher, 2004.

Jackson, Kay. *Explore the Desert*. Mankato, Minn.: Capstone Press, 2007.

Pfeffer, Wendy. *Hot Deserts*. New York: Benchmark Books, 2002.

Trumbauer, Lisa. *What Are Deserts?* Mankato, Minn.: Pebble Books, 2002.

Internet Addresses

Desert from the Missouri Botanical Garden
<http://www.mbgnet.net/sets/desert/index.htm>

The Desert Biome from the University of California Museum of Paleontology
<http://www.ucmp.berkeley.edu/exhibits/>
Click on "The World's Biomes." Click on "Desert."

Index

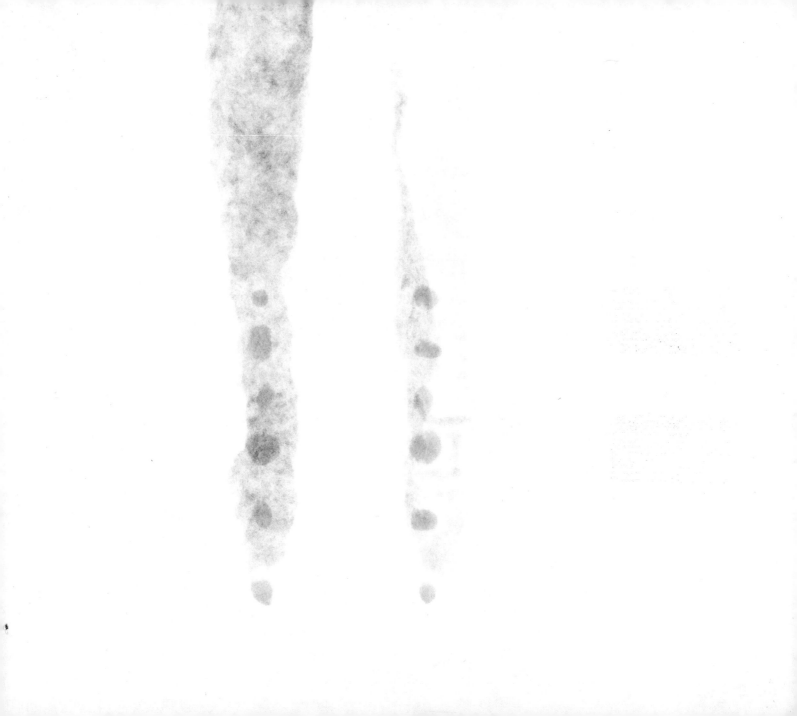